# Ironclads and Blockades in the Civil War

# Untold History of the Civil War

CHELSEA HOUSE PUBLISHERS

*Untold History of the Civil War*

# Ironclads and Blockades in the Civil War

*Douglas J. Savage*

CHELSEA HOUSE PUBLISHERS
Philadelphia

Produced by Combined Publishing
P.O. Box 307, Conshohocken, Pennsylvania 19428
1-800-418-6065
E-mail:combined@combinedpublishing.com
web:www.combinedpublishing.com

CHELSEA HOUSE PUBLISHERS

Editor in Chief: Stephen Reginald
Managing Editor: James D. Gallagher
Production Manager: Pamela Loos
Art Director: Sara Davis
Director of Photography: Judy L. Hasday
Senior Production Editor: LeeAnne Gelletly
Assistant Editor: Anne Hill

Front Cover Illustration: "The *Monitor* and the *Merrimack* at Short Range." Courtesy of the Franklin D. Roosevelt Library.

The Chelsea House World Wide Web site address is
http://www.chelseahouse.com

First Printing

135798642

Library of Congress Cataloging-in-Publication Data applied for:
ISBN 0-7910-5429-2

# Contents

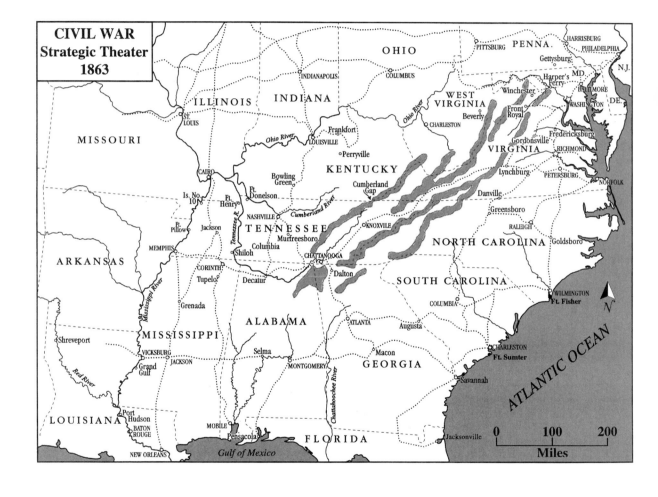

CIVIL WAR
Strategic Theater
1863

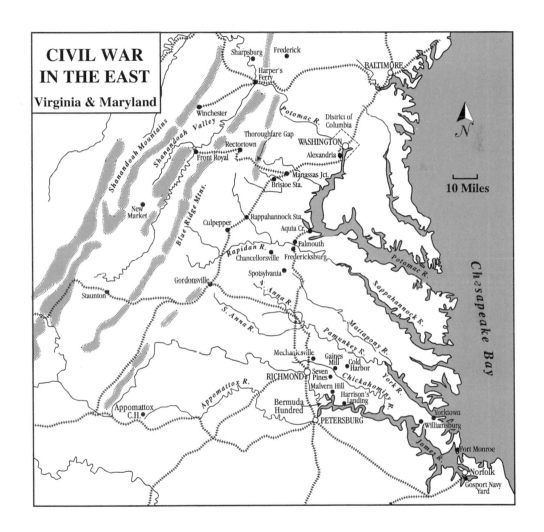

## CIVIL WAR IN THE EAST
### Virginia & Maryland

N

10 Miles

Shanandoah Mountains

Shanandoah Valley

Blue Ridge Mtns.

Sharpsburg
Frederick
Harper's Ferry
BALTIMORE
Winchester
Potomac R.
District of Columbia
Thoroughfare Gap
Rectortown
WASHINGTON
Front Royal
Alexandria
Manassas Jct.
Bristoe Sta.
New Market
Culpepper
Rappahannock Sta.
Aquia Cr.
Rapidan R.
Falmouth
Chancellorsville
Fredericksburg
Spotsylvania
Gordonsville
S. Anna R.
Anna R.
Staunton
Mattapony R.
Rappahannock R.
Potomac R.
Chesapeake Bay
Pamunkey R.
Mechanicsville
Gaines Mill
Cold Harbor
Seven Pines
RICHMOND
Chickahominy R.
Malvern Hill
Harrison's Landing
York R.
Appomattox R.
Bermuda Hundred
Yorktown
Appomattox C.H.
PETERSBURG
Williamsburg
James R.
Fort Monroe
Norfolk
Gosport Navy Yard

7

# Civil War Chronology

## 1860

**November 6**     Abraham Lincoln is elected president of the United States.

**December 20**     South Carolina becomes the first state to secede from the Union.

## 1861

**January-April**     Mississippi, Florida, Alabama, Georgia, Louisiana, and Texas also secede from the Union.

**April 1**     Bombardment of Fort Sumter begins the Civil War.

**April-May**     Lincoln calls for volunteers to fight the Southern rebellion, causing a second wave of secession with Virginia, Arkansas, Tennessee, and North Carolina all leaving the Union.

**May**     Union naval forces begin blockading the Confederate coast and reoccupying some Southern ports and offshore islands.

**July 21**     Union forces are defeated at the battle of First Bull Run and withdraw to Washington.

## 1862

**February**     Previously unknown Union general Ulysses S. Grant captures Confederate garrisons in Tennessee at Fort Henry (February 6) and Fort Donelson (February 16).

**March 7-8**     Confederates and their Cherokee allies are defeated at Pea Ridge, Arkansas.

**March 8-9**     Naval battle at Hampton Roads, Virginia, involving the USS *Monitor* and the CSS *Virginia* (formerly the USS *Merrimac*) begins the era of the armored fighting ship.

**April-July**     The Union army marches on Richmond after an amphibious landing. Confederate forces block Northern advance in a series of battles. Robert E. Lee is placed in command of the main Confederate army in Virginia.

**April 6-7**     Grant defeats the Southern army at Shiloh Church, Tennessee, after a costly two-day battle.

**April 27**     New Orleans is captured by Union naval forces under Admiral David Farragut.

**May 31**     The battle of Seven Pines (also called Fair Oaks) is fought and the Union lines are held.

**August 29-30**     Lee wins substantial victory over the Army of the Potomac at the battle of Second Bull Run near Manassas, Virginia.

**September 17**     Union General George B. McClellan repulses Lee's first invasion of the North at Antietam Creek near Sharpsburg, Maryland, in the bloodiest single day of the war.

**November 13**     Grant begins operations against the key Confederate fortress at Vicksburg, Mississippi.

**December 13**     Union forces suffer heavy losses storming Confederate positions at Fredericksburg, Virginia.

## 1863

**January 1**     President Lincoln issues the Emancipation Proclamation, freeing the slaves in the Southern states.

| | |
|---|---|
| **May 1-6** | Lee wins an impressive victory at Chancellorsville, but key Southern commander Thomas J. "Stonewall" Jackson dies of wounds, an irreplaceable loss for the Army of Northern Virginia. |
| **June** | The city of Vicksburg and the town of Port Hudson are held under siege by the Union army. They surrender on July 4. |
| **July 1-3** | Lee's second invasion of the North is decisively defeated at Gettysburg, Pennsylvania. |
| **July 16** | Union forces led by the black 54th Massachusetts Infantry attempt to regain control of Fort Sumter by attacking the Fort Wagner outpost. |
| **September 19-20** | Confederate victory at Chickamauga, Georgia, gives some hope to the South after disasters at Gettysburg and Vicksburg. |

## 1864

| | |
|---|---|
| **February 17** | A new Confederate submarine, the *Hunley,* attacks and sinks the USS *Housatonic* in the waters off Charleston. |
| **March 9** | General Grant is made supreme Union commander. He decides to campaign in the East with the Army of the Potomac while General William T. Sherman carries out a destructive march across the South from the Mississippi to the Atlantic coast. |
| **May-June** | In a series of costly battles (Wilderness, Spotsylvania, and Cold Harbor), Grant gradually encircles Lee's troops in the town of Petersburg, Richmond's railway link to the rest of the South. |
| **June 19** | The siege of Petersburg begins, lasting for nearly a year until the end of the war. |
| **August 27** | General Sherman captures Atlanta and begins the "March to the Sea," a campaign of destruction across Georgia and South Carolina. |
| **November 8** | Abraham Lincoln wins reelection, ending hope of the South getting a negotiated settlement. |
| **November 30** | Confederate forces are defeated at Franklin, Tennessee, losing five generals. Nashville is soon captured (December 15-16). |

## 1865

| | |
|---|---|
| **April 2** | Major Petersburg fortifications fall to the Union, making further resistance by Richmond impossible. |
| **April 3-8** | Lee withdraws his army from Richmond and attempts to reach Confederate forces still holding out in North Carolina. Union armies under Grant and Sheridan gradually encircle him. |
| **April 9** | Lee surrenders to Grant at Appomattox, Virginia, effectively ending the war. |
| **April 14** | Abraham Lincoln is assassinated by John Wilkes Booth, a Southern sympathizer. |

### Union Army
Army of the Potomac
Army of the James
Army of the Cumberland

### Confederate Army
Army of Northern Virginia
Army of Tennessee

*The USS* Essex *was one of the largest of the ironclads built during the Civil War.*

# I

# To Build a Navy

For 74 years of nationhood, the United States Constitution failed to resolve the question of slavery in our country. After 40 years of failed efforts by Congress to create patchwork compromises to prevent slavery from destroying the young country, civil war exploded at last in April 1861. Nearly one million men and boys from both the North and South would die from wounds or disease to finally settle the questions of slavery. With the coming of the Civil War, both the United States of America and the new Confederate States of America had millions of young men to fill their armies. But neither side had navies adequate for the bloodbath of "total war" which would last four years.

The United States government believed that its navy had kept up with the times after its victory in the 1847 Mexican War through the coming of the Civil War in 1861. Slowly, the old navy of "iron men on wooden ships" had gone from wooden ships powered by sails to a new and modern fleet powered by steam engines. But the new age of steam was not quite a complete change from the age of sail. The

United States Navy floated somewhere in-between, with its ocean-going warships carrying masts and sails *and* steam-driven propellers. These were "tall ships" which used their sails when their newfangled steam engines failed, which was often.

When the Civil War began, the navy had 44 steam-powered ships of which only six were "screw frigates" carrying both sail and steam-powered propellers. All six of these modern warships were built in 1855. The most famous of these would soon be the steamship *Merrimack*. The other steam-powered ships were adaptations of the familiar Mississippi River steamboats powered by paddle wheels. Most of the navy's non-sail steamships had two steam engines, each driving a separate paddle wheel mounted on each side of the ship.

*The USS* Eutaw, *a side-wheel streamer, built at the Washington Navy Yard during the Civil War.*

But every one of the United States Navy's 44 modern steamships was wooden. Not one was covered with iron armor. Because of this, on a single, beautiful spring morning one year into the war, the entire United States Navy would become completely obsolete.

*During the Civil War, Stephen R. Mallory served as Secretary of the Confederate Navy.*

In March 1861, President Lincoln nominated 50-year-old Gideon Welles to his cabinet as Secretary of the Navy. A Connecticut native, Welles began his political life as a Democrat. He then joined the Republican Party and played an important role in Lincoln's winning the 1860 Republican presidential nomination. Before becoming part of Lincoln's wartime cabinet, Welles had been a newspaperman and owner of the *Hartford Times* in Connecticut.

Naval Secretary Welles worked hard to expand and modernize the United States Navy. Between March and December 1861, he recommissioned 76 retired ships, purchased 136 new ones, and built another 52, to expand the service to 264 ships. Like the army before the war, the navy also had to recruit and train thousands of officers and seamen. When the war began, the navy had only 1,457 officers and 7,600 sailors. Four years later, the U.S. Navy had 7,500 officers and 51,500 sailors. Also like the Federal army at the beginning of the war, the navy lost many qualified seamen and officers who resigned from the Federal navy to offer their services to the South. Over 322 U.S. Navy officers joined the Confederate navy.

At least the United States in 1861 had a real navy with a heroic tradition going back 85 years to the American Revolution. The Confederate States of America had no navy at all in 1861. The new country's national government in Richmond, Virginia, had to buy or build a navy out of nothing. So within the first year of the Civil War, the Confederacy bought or rebuilt 44 riverboats for combat. Richmond also built 24 new steamships, mostly sidewheeler, wooden ships like the pre-war United States Navy. Stephen Mallory, a former judge and United States senator from Florida, served as secretary of the new Confederate navy. While in the U.S. Senate, Mallory had been chairman of the Committee on Naval Affairs. By war's end in 1865, Secretary Mallory would be the only Confederate cabinet secretary who served the entire war in one department.

Both Rebel Secretary Mallory and Yankee Secretary Welles understood that the American Civil War would be the first truly modern war. Both men knew that wooden ships, under sail or steam power, would soon be useless antiques. Modern, 19th-century artillery required warships with iron armor—"ironclads." Mallory commissioned the construction of two new ironclad warships for the Confederate navy, the

*Tennessee* and the *Arkansas*. Both Rebel ironclads were planned to defend the vital Mississippi River which cut the Confederacy down the middle.

In July 1861, Gideon Welles sent a message to the United States Congress requesting a board of naval experts to study ironclad developments. On August 3, Congress approved three experts and a budget of $1.5 million for ironclad research and construction. Secretary Welles called for warship construction proposals by September 9. Since these ships were also planned for river fighting, the navy set a limit of 16

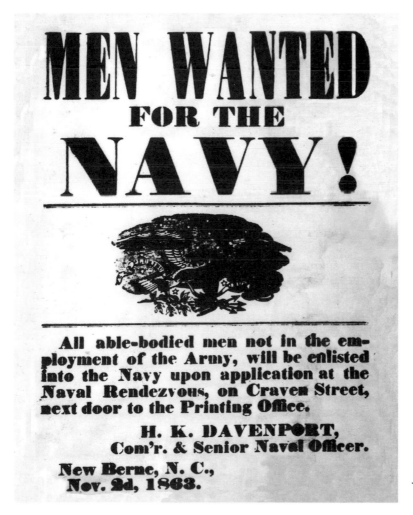

*Federal recruiting poster for the Union navy in 1863.*

feet on the new designs' "draft" which is how deep in the water a ship floats. A seagoing ship would have too much draft to sail shallow rivers.

The Congressional panel of naval experts issued their report to Secretary Welles on September 16, 1861. Although the experts believed in ironclad boats for a modern navy, they did not believe that ironclads would make stable and safe ships for ocean sailing. "As cruising vessels," the experts reported, "we are skeptical as to their advantages and ultimate adoption." In spite of such reservations, the U.S. Navy signed a contract on October 4, 1861, for its first new ironclad warship which would be called the USS *Monitor* and would change fighting at sea forever.

At the beginning of the war, the United States Navy had no interest in warfare on inland rivers. So the fight for the vital Mississippi River was left to the army. In August 1861, the army, not the navy, commissioned the building of seven new ironclad "gunboats" for river work. These ships were to have a single paddle wheel and their above-water sides were to be covered with two and one-half inches of iron armor. River gunboats with only one inch of iron armor were also commissioned. With lighter armor than the heavier gunboats, these were called "tinclads."

The United States Navy grew quickly. From 82 warships and gunboats in July 1861, the navy grew to 264 vessels by the end of the year, and to more than 600 ships by the end of the war. During the four years of naval fighting on rivers and at sea, 60 monitor-class ironclads were also built or planned for the Union navy.

The armor-covered gunboats went to war before the more famous and larger ironclads. The seven armored riverboats were built by James B. Eads of St. Louis. Since Eads worked with U. S. Navy builder Samuel M.

Pook, the new gunboats with their iron sides were called "Pook's turtles." The new turtles would be tested first at the northern mouth of the Mississippi River in early 1862.

Captain Andrew H. Foote of the United States Navy was given command of the Union's Mississippi River fleet. When the war began, the South controlled the vital river. President Lincoln's administration knew that the war could not be won without capturing the river which would cut the Confederacy in half.

During the first week of February 1862, Captain Foote put his new gunboats in the water at Cairo, Illinois. He had four of the boats ready for combat: the *Cincinnati*, the *Essex*, the *St. Louis*, and the *Carondelet*. Each was 175-feet long, 51-feet wide, and each had a draft of only 6 feet for sailing shallow rivers. Foote's expedition downriver would mark the first test of American-built ironclads in real combat.

Captain Foote had to use soldiers from the army as crewmen in his gunboats. The navy still was not ready to risk its prestige on a new invention. Captain Foote and his soldier-sailors headed east, up the Ohio River and then sailed south, "up" the Tennessee River into northwest Tennessee. The four Pook's turtles sailed with three troopships carrying 15,000 soldiers under the command of a new Yankee general named Ulysses Grant. Their mission was to capture Confederate Fort Henry on the Tennessee River and then Fort Donelson on the nearby Cumberland River.

*Captain Andrew H. Foote was placed in charge of the Union fleet on the Mississippi River in 1861.*

*Captain Foote's fleet depicted sailing on the Mississippi River in 1862.*

On February 6, 1862, Captain Foote's four paddle-wheel steamships aimed their 11 cannons at Fort Henry. The tiny navy's cannons pounded the fort for 85 minutes and came within 600 yards of the fort on the riverbank. The Rebels fired back with their own cannons. The *Essex* was hit by a cannon shell which entered an open gunport, killing one soldier and wounding 38. Captain Foote's own turtle, the *Cincinnati*, was hit 17 times, killing one soldier and wounding nine. The *St. Louis* was hit 7 times and the *Carondelet* was hit 6 times. But none of the iron-covered gunboats sank. Except for lucky shots going through open gunports, Rebel cannonballs and artillery shells simply bounced off the iron ships.

General Grant landed 15,000 infantry near Fort Henry and by 2:00 in the afternoon, Fort Henry surrendered. Ironclad warships, even those called turtles, had proved themselves unsinkable and deadly. A new age of naval warfare had begun on that sixth day of February in 1862 on the Tennessee River.

The little gunboat fleet was not quite so fortunate eight days later when General Grant's Yankees attacked the Rebel Fort Donelson on the Cumberland. On February 14, Captain Foote's fleet committed four ironclads, the *St. Louis*, the *Carondelet*, the *Louisville*, and the new *Pittsburgh*, plus two wooden gunboats. The ironclads pounded the fort for 90 minutes. The *Carondelet* was disabled when one of her own cannons exploded. In a ferocious artillery barrage from the Confederate fort, the other three ironclad gunboats were also disabled and Captain Foote was slightly wounded. Still, no ironclad gunboat had sunk and Fort Donelson surrendered on February 16 after a heroic, two-day struggle.

The ironclad action in Tennessee proved that the age of wooden warships was quickly ending. The age of ironclads was about to begin only three weeks later. Two warships named the *Virginia* and the *Monitor* permanently ended wooden navies on March 9, 1862.

*The officers of the USS* Monitor *in July of 1862.*

# II

# *The Monitor and the Virginia*

When the Civil War began in April 1861, the single most important harbor of the United States Navy was the Norfolk Navy Yard in Virginia, on the Portsmouth side of the Elizabeth River. The navy yard covered almost one mile of riverfront and reached inland another mile.

Virginia left the Union on April 17. The next day, Virginia's Governor John Letcher ordered the Virginia militia to capture the navy yard for the Confederacy. The federal officer defending the Norfolk Navy Yard was Commodore Charles McCauley, 68 years old and a navy man for 50 years. Naval Secretary Gideon Welles ordered Commodore McCauley to get the United States Navy's new wooden steamship, the USS *Merrimack*, ready to escape as soon as possible, before the Rebels attacked Norfolk. The *Merrimack* was 375 feet long and she was armed with two gun decks. Like her sister ships, she was a steam frigate powered by two steam engines and full sail. The *Merrimack* was stuck at her dock undergoing repairs. Yankee workmen labored night and day to make her ready for sailing north.

Work at the navy yard continued at a feverish pace throughout April 18 and 19. President Lincoln sent 349 soldiers and 100 United States Marines to the yard to defend its huge supply of naval cannons and its 10 warships—the *Merrimack* being the most important. But in the face of approaching Rebel troops, Commodore McCauley froze. The old sailor did not order his one prized warship to sail for safety. Instead, he ordered the *Merrimack* burned and sunk so she would not fall into Confederate hands.

On April 21, 1861, the Federals evacuated Norfolk Navy Yard and left behind the smoldering hulk of the *Merrimack*, sunk and burned to the waterline, and 1,198 naval cannons which the Confederacy would use against the United States for the next four years. Among the abandoned artillery were 52 nine-inch Dahlgren guns, the United States Navy's most modern naval weapons.

The loss of the navy yard and the *Merrimack* was a Federal disaster which would get worse.

Confederate Secretary of the Navy Stephen Mallory wasted no time. He ordered Rebel engineers to salvage the *Merrimack* wreck, save what they could, and use the hulk as the foundation for the South's first ironclad warship.

The Confederates raised the *Merrimack* and built on her hull a massive, armored fortress. Her upper deck was rebuilt from solid oak, 21-inches thick. On top of that, engineers laid four inches of iron armor. The armored deck casement was shorter than the *Merrimack*'s length, so the rest of the old wooden hull would protrude almost under water ahead of and behind the armored deck. An iron ram which weighed 1,500 pounds was mounted to her front end. The ram was designed to be driven by the *Merrimack*'s twin steam engines into the sides of wooden Yankee ships.

There would be no masts and no sails. This was an armored, steam-powered, propeller-driven warship like nothing ever seen on the water.

Confederate naval engineer John L. Porter worked on the *Merrimack* for 10 months. When he was finished, the *Merrimack*'s full length had been shortened to 275 feet. The armored upper deck covered 160 feet of her length. The sides of the upper deck were sloped inward at 36-degree angles to deflect artillery shells and solid cannonballs. The iron ram was totally submerged and jutted out 50 feet forward of the armored deck. Ten cannons were mounted in the armored deck. Six of the heavy guns were 9-inch Dahlgren cannons abandoned by the fleeing Yankees.

The *Merrimack* was ready to sail in March 1862. But first, she was christened with a new Rebel name: the CSS *Virginia*. Captain Franklin Buchanan took command of the new *Virginia* with Lieutenant Catesby Jones as his executive officer. Captain Buchanan was 61 years old and had spent his entire life in the United States Navy. He was the first superintendent of the United States Naval Academy. A Maryland native, Captain Buchanan went South when war came.

*The USS* Merrimack *was salvaged by the Confederate navy and made into the ironclad CSS* Virginia *(above).*

*This sketch of the CSS* Virginia's *attack on the* USS Cumberland *was printed in* Harper's Weekly *in March of 1862.*

Too many history books refer to the *Virginia* by her earlier name, the *Merrimack*. Since she sailed during the Civil War under the Confederate flag, she should bear her honored Rebel name, the *Virginia*.

On March 8, the *Virginia* left Norfolk Naval Yard and sailed for the United States naval yard at Hampton Roads, Virginia. Captain Buchanan gave his Confederate sailors their last order before battle, "Sink before surrender."

Making way into Hampton Roads on the 8th, the *Virginia* was challenged by four Yankee warships, the steam-powered and all-wood *Minnesota* and *Roanoke*, and two wooden sailing warships, the *Cumberland* and the *Congress*. The age of iron collided with the age of wood and sail. At 1:00, the *Virginia* headed into Hampton Roads. When the *Virginia* began firing her 10 cannons, she used gunpowder which had been abandoned on board the old *Merrimack*.

At 2:30, the *Virginia* aimed her iron, submerged ram at the wooden frigate *Cumberland*. She slammed into the *Cumberland* so hard that the *Virginia*'s iron ram broke off when it crushed the *Cumberland*'s wooden side. The *Cumberland* never had a chance against iron. On board the *Virginia*, Lieutenant John Taylor Wood could see that "our ram had opened her side wide enough to drive in a horse and cart. . . . The side of the *Cumberland* was crushed like an egg shell."

As water flooded the *Cumberland*, her 376 brave sailors continued to fire their cannons at the *Virginia*. The cannonballs bounced from the ironclad's sides. The Yankee sailors continued firing even as they sank. The *Virginia*'s executive officer, Lieutenant Catesby Jones, remembered 25 years later that "The *Cumberland* fought her guns gallantly as long as they were above water and she went down bravely with her colors flying."

On the Virginia shore, hundreds of civilians watched the grim naval battle. Strangely, they saw the deadly struggle, but they heard nothing. A strong wind blew the sounds of cannons away from the spectators.

With the *Cumberland* sunk, the *Virginia* turned to ram the *Congress*. The sailing ship managed to escape, but her bottom grounded in shallow water. She was stuck. The *Virginia* fired at her from open water. Twenty-five years later, James Russell Soley described the scene as the *Virginia* pounded the beached *Congress*: "Her decks were covered with the dead and dying; her commander was killed, and fire had broken out in different parts of the ship. The affair had ceased to be a fight; it was simply a wholesale slaughter."

Still beached, the *Congress* surrendered. Of her crew, 136 were dead or wounded. The *Virginia*'s Captain Buchanan could take little pleasure in his second defeated Yankee ship of the afternoon: Captain Buchanan's brother was an officer on the *Congress*.

At 5:00 in the evening, March 8, 1862, the *Virginia* sailed out of Hampton Roads. Behind her, she left the *Cumberland* sunk and the *Congress* burning. The

Yankee fleet had fought hard and had killed or wounded 21 men on board the *Virginia*. But the Rebel ironclad had lived to escape and she also left behind 400 dead and wounded Federals.

The *Virginia* sailed back toward Norfolk, certain that she had ended the United States Navy's role in the Civil War. Captain Buchanan could not have known that Naval Secretary Welles was as farsighted as Confederate Secretary Mallory. Even as the *Virginia* sailed away on March 8, a Yankee ironclad was sailing toward Hampton Roads to even the score.

When the Federal, congressional experts approved construction of the Union's first ironclad warship, in the fall of 1861, shipbuilder Cornelius Bushnell went to the nautical inventor John Ericsson. Bushnell learned that Ericsson had already built a wooden model of a totally new type of warship, armored with iron. Bushnell took the model to Navy Secretary Welles who was sufficiently impressed to show the model to President Lincoln.

*Sailors on board the USS* Monitor *in July of 1862.*

Secretary Welles authorized Ericsson to build one ship and to build it fast—in only 100 days. Ericsson laid the keel of his new ship at the Greenpoint, Long Island, New York, ship yard in October 1861 and he launched his revolutionary design on January 30, 1862. Ericsson named his ship the *Monitor*.

The USS *Monitor* had a hull 124 feet long and 34 feet wide. The hull rode beneath the waterline. On top, Ericsson built a 174-foot-long raft, which was 5 feet high and covered with 5 inches of iron plates. Perched in the middle of the raft was a single gun turret covered with 8 inches of iron plate. Inside the 9-foot-tall, 20-foot-wide turret, Ericsson mounted two 11-inch Dahlgren cannons. With the raft barely rising above the waterline, witnesses called the *Monitor* a floating cheese box. Out on the front bow of the *Monitor*, Ericsson set the pilot-house, four feet high with nine inches of iron armor and room for three men. From here, the ship's captain would steer the warship. The whole turret revolved in a circular track, so the two cannons could fire in any direction—except straight ahead which would blow up the forward pilothouse. Each cannon required so much work to load, aim, and fire that eight sailors were assigned to each gun.

When a panel of experts met in August 1861 and authorized the experimental ironclad, they had serious concerns that ironclads would not be seaworthy. The *Monitor* proved them right, twice.

When the Rebel ironclad *Virginia* sailed for Hampton Roads, the *Monitor* was already sailing from New York to Hampton Roads. She was so unseaworthy and so difficult to steer on the open ocean that she had to be towed the whole way by the Union ship *Rhode Island*. In the rush to build a navy, the Union had purchased the steamship *Eagle* in July 1861 and refitted her to become a warship. With two side-mounted paddle wheels and eight 8-inch cannons, the 236-foot-long *Eagle* was renamed the *Rhode Island*.

For three harrowing days, the *Rhode Island* towed the lumbering cheese box on a raft toward Hampton Roads, Virginia. When strong wind caused rough seas, the *Monitor* almost sank in the swells rolling over her main deck, which were nearly level with the water. The *Monitor*'s 22-year-old executive officer, Lieutenant S. Dana Greene, remembered that nauseating trip 25 years later: "Nothing but the subsidence of the wind prevented her from being shipwrecked before we reached Hampton Roads."

With Captain John Worden in the pilothouse under the shadow of the iron turret behind him, the *Monitor* reached Hampton Roads at 9:00 on the night of March 8, 1862. Her way into the harbor was illuminated by the burning wreck of the USS *Congress*. Four and a half hours later, the *Congress* exploded when her gun powder magazines burned. The *Virginia* had destroyed two Union ships.

At dawn on Sunday, March 9, the CSS *Virginia* returned to Hampton Roads to finish her bloody work—she came back to sink the beached Yankee warship *Minnesota*. Beside the *Virginia* was her Confederate support ship the *Patrick Henry*. Before the war, the *Patrick Henry* had been the private steamship the *Yorktown*. Now, she was also the floating Confederate States Naval Academy.

The *Virginia*'s crew was surprised to see another ironclad steaming toward her. The *Monitor*'s Captain Worden was 44 years old and had spent 28 years in the United States Navy. He had already been a prisoner of war of the Confederates and he was not about to be captured again.

The ironclads aimed for each other at 8:00 in the morning. When less than one mile apart, the *Monitor*'s two cannons fired.

Just as the *Virginia*'s captain had a brother on board the destroyed USS *Congress*, the battle between the *Virginia* and the *Monitor* was a fight between old friends: Lieutenant Waller Butt on the *Virginia* was the United States Naval Academy roommate of the *Monitor*'s Lieutenant Dana Greene.

The two ironclads pounded each other for the next four hours. Neither ship was firing solid cannonballs, but hollow shells with timed fuses. Each ship was engulfed in exploding shells and flying shrapnel. The iron fragments bounced off each ship's armor. In the *Monitor*'s revolving turret, Lieutenant Greene had to be very careful not to fire his twin cannons into the back of the pilothouse on the *Monitor*'s bow. During the four-hour battle, the ironclads bumped into each other many times. The *Virginia*'s cannons fired almost directly into the peep holes of the *Monitor*'s little pilothouse. Captain Worden was blinded by gunpowder flakes and flying splinters of wood. Young Lieutenant Greene took over command of the ship. Twenty-five years later, he remembered his wounded captain's face: "He was a ghastly sight, with his eyes closed and the blood apparently rushing from every pore in the upper part of his face."

But neither ironclad was badly damaged. By 4:00, the *Virginia* had had enough and steered out of Hampton Roads. The *Monitor* had been hit by 21 shells, including seven hits on her round turret. But the shells only made dents, some as deep as four inches.

*The famous battle between the USS* Monitor *and the refurbished CSS* Virginia *took place in March of 1862.*

The Confederacy regarded the Hampton Roads battle between ironclads as a victory. Confederate President Jefferson Davis called it a "brilliant triumph" on April 10, 1862. Three days earlier, his Navy Secretary Mallory wrote that the CSS *Virginia* "achieved the most remarkable victory which naval annals record."

Historians have debated who won since March 9, 1862. The facts remain that the *Virginia* destroyed two United States warships on March 8, but she failed to destroy the USS *Minnesota* when she returned the next day. Nor did she sink or seriously damage the USS *Monitor*. Likewise, the *Monitor* did not sink or seriously damage the *Virginia*.

One month later, on April 11, 1862, the *Virginia* sailed back into Hampton Roads. But the *Monitor* was still there protecting the United States fleet, along with the USS *Vanderbilt*, a navy ship designed for ramming. The *Virginia* turned around and withdrew without a shot. She was never put to sea again.

The *Monitor*'s Captain Worden was hospitalized in Washington for the wounds to his face. The men and boys of the *Monitor*—every one a volunteer for the new ship—loved Captain Worden. They sent him a longhand letter at the hospital: "These few lines is [sic] from your own crew of the *Monitor*, with their kindest love to you, their honored captain, hoping to God that they will have the pleasure of welcoming you back to us again soon."

On May 10, 1862, Union forces laid siege to Norfolk Navy Yard to win it back. The ironclad *Virginia* was still docked there and could not escape. President Lincoln ordered the *Monitor* to bombard Confederate positions near Norfolk. Before dawn on May 11, Confederates burned the heroic CSS *Virginia* to prevent her capture by the Yankees. For the second time in 13 months, the old hulk of the USS *Merrimack* was burned and scuttled.

The *Virginia* exploded at 4:58 in the morning on May 11. From the deck of the steamship USS *Baltimore*, Abraham Lincoln watched her burn and sink.

In December, the USS *Rhode Island* sailed to Hampton Roads to tow the unseaworthy *Monitor* down the coast. During the first minutes of New Year's eve 1862, the *Monitor* was so unstable in rough seas that the *Rhode Island* had to cut her loose before she sank both ships. The USS *Monitor* sank just after midnight December 31, near Cape Hatteras. Sixteen sailors went to the bottom with her.

By the end of 1862, the two ships which ended the age of sail were both gone.

*The Confederate ironclad* Stonewall.

III

# The Achilles Heal: Wooden Bottoms

*D*espite the success of both the *Virginia* and the *Monitor* and the new age of ironclad warships which they introduced, the Civil War on the water demonstrated the ironclads' two greatest failures. They were ironclad ships with wooden hulls and they were not useful warships against land fortifications. Ironclads were not battleships, or "dreadnaughts" as they would be called by World War I in 1914.

One year after the duel of ironclads at Hampton Roads, the U. S. Navy was overconfident that its new ironclads like the *Monitor* could destroy forts on shore. Rear Admiral C. R. P. Rogers wrote in 1887: "The most dramatic conflict between the *Monitor* and the *Merrimack* . . . gave to the Navy Department the hope that its turret vessels might do what unarmored ships could not attempt." In April 1863, Admiral Samuel F. DuPont would attempt to recapture Fort Sumter in Charleston Harbor, South Carolina. The 59-year-old

admiral, had been in the United States Navy since he was 12.

Expecting attack by sea, gunners at Fort Sumter used floating buoys in Charleston Harbor to mark distances for aiming their 44 cannons. Another seven forts along the harbor mouth aimed 77 cannons at the water. If a Yankee ship sailed near any buoy, the Confederate cannoneers could set the preselected ranges of their guns precisely for that distance. On April 7, 1863, nine Union ironclads were towed into Charleston Harbor for the attack against Fort Sumter. At 1:15 in the afternoon, they entered the bay in single file. The little fleet of seven monitor-class cheese boxes and two armored steamships carried 23 cannons. Fort Sumter's cannons began firing at 2:50. In just 40 minutes, the ironclad USS *Weehawken* was hit 53 times. After being hit 35 times by Rebel cannon, the USS *Passaic*'s iron turret was disabled. The *Monitor*'s wounded Captain John Worden was back in action as captain of the USS *Montauk*. She was hit 14 times. The ironclad USS *Patapsco* was hit 47 times; the USS

*Part of the Union's ironclad navy was featured in* Harper's Weekly *in September 1862. (From left to right: the* Puritan, *the* Woodna, *the* Roanoke, *the* Ironsides, *the* Naugatauk, *and the* Monitor.)

*Catskill* was hit 20 times; the flagship of Admiral DuPont, the *New Ironsides*, was hit 65 times; the USS *Nahant* was hit 36 times; and the tiny, newest ironclad, the USS *Keokuk*, took 90 hits.

The fleet pounded Fort Sumter with 139 rounds of cannon fire. The fort was only hit 55 times. But the fort rained down 2,229 rounds of cannon fire onto the fleet. In the smoke and confusion, the flagship *New Ironsides* collided twice with two of the little monitor-class ships, without serious damage to either.

With all of the Yankee ironclads still afloat, the fleet withdrew from the attack as the sun set behind the cloud of smoke. That evening at 5:00, every captain from the fleet's nine ironclads told Admiral DuPont that their ships were too badly damaged to fight another day. Admiral DuPont canceled the next day's attack on Fort Sumter. The double-turret ironclad *Keokuk* sank the next morning.

Captain Daniel Ammen of the ironclad *Patapsco* wrote of the Charleston raid 20 years later: "The damage inflicted on the vessels shows that they were inca-

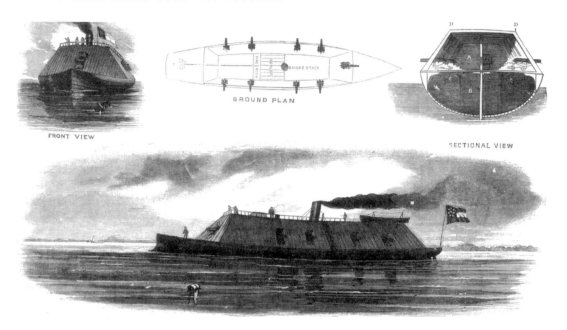

FRONT VIEW

GROUND PLAN

SECTIONAL VIEW

*Sketches of the CSS* Richmond *with four different views made by a sailor aboard the USS* Teazer.

pable of enduring heavy blows sufficiently long to effect the destruction of Sumter." The Charleston attack in April 1863 confirmed that Civil War ironclads were not yet battleships.

Eighteen months later, the weakness of ironclads built with wooden bottoms was demonstrated by the Confederate ironclad CSS *Albemarle*, which resembled the *Virginia*: a tall, iron-covered casement mounted on a wooden "raft." She was 122 feet long and 45 feet wide. Her armored upper deck was 60 feet long, covered with four inches of iron. Inside the upper deck were two cannons, one at each end, which could swivel through half a circle. Steam engines turned two propellers.

The *Albemarle* steamed down the Roanoke River toward Albemarle Sound, North Carolina, on April 18, 1864. The Confederate ironclad confronted the Yankee steamers *Miami* and *Southfield*. Neither was an ironclad. The *Albemarle* rammed the *Southfield* so hard that the iron ram on the *Albemarle*'s bow stuck in the *Southfield*'s wooden side. Had the *Southfield* not rolled over when she sank, snapping off the ram, she would have dragged the *Albemarle* under with her.

The *Albemarle* then steamed toward the *Miami*. The Union ship fired her cannons. The ships were so close to each other that a shell from one of the *Miami*'s cannons bounced off the Rebel ironclad's side, spun back into the *Miami*, and killed the *Miami*'s captain, C. W. Flusser. The Federal sidewheeler managed to escape downriver before the *Albemarle* could ram her.

For the next six months, the ram *Albemarle* threatened Yankee shipping on the Roanoke River. On the night of October 27, 1864, United States Navy Lieutenant William B. Cushing and seven volunteers took a small boat up the Roanoke River to destroy the *Albemarle*. Cushing's boat carried a 14-foot-long mast which could be tipped forward into the water. On the end of the mast hung a "torpedo"—a can of gunpowder with an ignition cap.

In the darkness, with Confederate rifles firing at him from shore, Lieutenant Cushing found the Rebel ironclad at anchor, surrounded by a barricade of floating logs. Cushing drove his boat on top of the slippery logs, lowered his mast with the torpedo attached, and detonated the little bomb under the ram's wooden bottom. The *Albemarle*'s captain, Alexander Warley, felt his ship shudder at the blast. He sent a seaman down to check the damage. The ship's carpenter reported "a hole in her bottom big enough to drive a wagon in."

The CSS *Albemarle* sank quickly, due to her wooden bottom. Cushing and his men swam downriver to safety. The Cushing family had already made one sacrifice for its country before the sinking of the *Albemarle*. Cushing's brother had been killed at Gettysburg in July 1863. Now another Cushing was a hero, but he had survived.

Two months before Lieutenant Cushing sank the *Albemarle*, the United States Navy proved that ironclads could make it past coastal forts, if the ships kept moving. But the Union navy also learned the hazard of wooden bottoms on ironclads.

Civil War ironclads, whether monitor-class turret boats, *Virginia*-style "rafts" with armored casements on the nearly submerged raft, or armorplated, paddlewheel steamships, were all built on top of old-fashioned wood hulls. The wooden sides usually ended at the waterline. A lucky, solid cannonball aimed right at the waterline could miss the heavy armor and strike vulnerable wood, sinking even the most sturdy ironclads.

After the Yankees captured New Orleans, the most important Confederate harbor on the Gulf of Mexico was Mobile, Alabama. In August 1864, U. S. Admiral David Farragut tried to run his fleet into Mobile Bay, past two Confederate forts on each side of the harbor entrance.

For the run past the forts, Admiral Farragut assembled a fleet of 19 warships which included four *Monitor*-type ironclads. Army signalmen were stationed on the ships to communicate by signal flags ship-to-ship. One such soldier was Lieutenant John Kinney, assigned to Admiral Farragut's flagship, *Hartford*, a steamship but not an ironclad. Kinney would remember Admiral Farragut's old face as "an expression combining overflowing kindliness with iron will and determination."

On August 4, 1864, the old admiral scouted Mobile Bay. Rebel Fort Gaines guarded one side of the harbor, three miles from the shoreline. That was too far from the water to be much trouble. But on the right side of the bay, Fort Morgan sat on the water's edge with three rows of deadly cannons. Inside Mobile Bay was Farragut's worst enemy: the ironclad ram CSS *Tennessee*. Built at Selma, Alabama, she was protected by six inches of iron plate and she carried six cannons. Her iron battering ram bow could sink any of Farragut's dozen wooden-hulled warships as easily as the CSS *Virginia* had sunk the USS *Cumberland* at Hampton Roads.

Admiral Farragut hoped to seal the bay so Confederate blockade-runners could no longer bring in supplies, destroy the CSS *Tennessee*, and isolate Rebel troops who would be trapped in the two forts if the Yankee fleet could enter and hold the harbor.

The Federal fleet included two kinds of monitor-class ironclads. The *Tecumseh* and the *Manhattan* were like the *Monitor* with a single turret containing two 15-inch cannons. The *Winnebago* and the *Chickasaw* were newer ships with double turrets giving each ship four 11-inch guns.

On August 5, 1864, Admiral Farragut steamed into Mobile Bay at 5:45 in the morning. The four ironclads led the way, followed by seven steam-powered paddle wheelers.

The admiral could not see the action from the *Hartford* behind the ironclads because of the gun smoke. So he climbed his steamer's rope rigging. A sailor lashed the old admiral to the rigging with a

*Rear Admiral David G. Farragut led the Union fleet during the battle of Mobile Bay.*

*Explosive charges, or torpedoes as they were called at the time, such as these were placed in the rivers as part of blockades.*

rope. Fort Morgan poured heavy fire onto the Yankee fleet entering the harbor.

The monitor-class *Tecumseh* quickly sailed into an underwater mine. During the Civil War, explosive charges were suspended under water like modern mines. At the time, they were called torpedoes. The *Tecumseh* struck such a gunpowder-filled torpedo. It destroyed her wooden bottom and she sank quickly, taking Captain Tunis Craven and 92 men to the bottom of Mobile Bay. The *Tecumseh*'s loss demonstrated the cheese box's weak spot: their wood hulls beneath the waterline.

Even in the American Civil War's vicious bloodshed, there were still gentlemen. When the flagship *Hartford* stopped her engines to pick up the *Tecumseh*'s 21 survivors, Confederate General Richard L. Page at Fort Morgan ordered his gunners to stop firing on the *Hartford* during the rescue. Before the war, General

Page had been a sailor and he had sailed with Admiral Farragut.

The land cannons heavily damaged the wooden steamers in the Yankee fleet. On the *Hartford*, army signalman, Lieutenant John Kinney, never forgot the scene. "The sight on deck was sickening beyond the power of words to portray. Shot after shot came through the side, mowing down the men, deluging the decks with blood and scattering mangled fragments of humanity so thickly that it was difficult to stand on the deck, so slippery was it."

After picking up the *Tecumseh*'s survivors, the battered *Hartford* and the fleet pushed into the harbor. More floating mines lay ahead. When a sailor warned the admiral hanging from the rigging about the floating explosives, Admiral Farragut shouted his immortal words, "Damn the torpedoes! Full speed ahead."

Keeping their steam up, the heavily damaged Yankee fleet managed to sail past the two forts and enter the harbor. Once the Federals sailed past the dangerous forts, the ironclad ram *Tennessee* attacked the fleet.

*The ironclad ram CSS* Tennessee *fought bravely at the battle of Mobile Bay.*

The brave men on the *Tennessee* sailed out to single-handedly attack the entire Yankee squadron of 10 wooden steamers and three surviving ironclads. The *Tennessee* managed to ram the Yankee steamships *Monongahela* and *Lackawanna*, but she did little damage. Then the Rebel ram collided with the *Hartford* but failed to hit her squarely enough to penetrate the flagship's wooden hull. As the ships touched, the *Tennessee* fired one of her cannons into the *Hartford*'s side, killing five seamen and wounding eight.

Surrounded by the federal fleet, the CSS *Tennessee* finally surrendered when her brave captain was wounded—Captain Franklin Buchanan who had skippered the *Virginia* into Hampton Roads in March 1862.

Mobile Bay was captured. But the United States Navy had lost 145 men and had 170 wounded. Two Confederate sailors on the *Tennessee* were killed and nine wounded.

Mobile Bay proved the risk of wooden bottoms on ironclads, but also proved that ironclads could run past short cannons. Nevertheless, the actual city of Mobile was never captured, only the harbor. Confederate Fort Morgan at the water's edge held out for another two weeks, and the city of Mobile held out until three days after Robert E. Lee surrendered in April 1865.

The capture of Mobile Bay ended that port's participation in the Confederacy's four-year effort to beat the Yankee navy's blockade of Southern seaports.

Historians have argued that running the Yankee blockade was the only siege the Confederacy ever won during the Civil War.

# IV

# *Blockades and Blockade-Runners*

*A*braham Lincoln became the 16th president of the United States on March 4, 1861. By that day, the federal Union had already dissolved as Southern states began leaving the Union. Fort Sumter in Charleston Harbor, South Carolina, fell to the Confederacy on April 14, 1861.

The next day, President Lincoln asked for 75,000 volunteers for the Union armies being formed and trained. In response, on April 17, Confederate President Jefferson Davis issued "letters of marque" giving Southern ships the authority to become "privateers" or raiders of Union civilian merchant ships.

Two days later, President Lincoln issued a proclamation decreeing a blockade of those Southern ports which faced the Atlantic Ocean and the Gulf of Mexico. The blockade proclamation of April 19 only blockaded the seaports of those Southern states which had thus far left the Union: South Carolina, Georgia, Alabama, Florida, Mississippi, Louisiana, and Texas.

President Lincoln knew that Confederate ships were now authorized to seize Union ships on the high seas, even though the Confederacy still had no serious navy of its own. Lincoln's April 19th proclamation took careful aim at such privateers: "I hereby proclaim and declare that if any person, under the pretended authority of the said States, or under any other pretense, shall molest a vessel of the United States, or the persons or cargo on board of her, such person will be held amenable to the laws of the United States for the prevention and punishment of piracy."

Under international law, the very word "piracy" is heavy with legal meaning. Pirates are international criminals who may be executed upon capture. President Lincoln was making a very deliberate threat that Confederate seamen who attempted to capture Union merchant ships would be hanged as pirates.

President Jefferson Davis did not blink. He quickly announced that Yankee sailors who interfered with Confederate ships would also be hanged as pirates. But Lincoln and Davis quietly backed away from any talk of enforcing piracy penalties and no one was hanged for piracy during the Civil War. Each side finally agreed that Confederate and Union sailors caught raiding the other's shipping would be prisoners of war instead of pirates. Lincoln's second blockade proclamation of April 27 did not mention piracy.

The presidential blockade proclamation announced Washington's intent to prevent all merchant shipping from entering or leaving Confederate seaports. Washington hoped to strangle the Confederacy's war effort by cutting off the sale of Southern cotton to Europe, especially to England, and by stopping the South's purchase of weapons, ammunition, and food from abroad. The Federal blockade was designed to

*The USS* Minnesota *was the flagship of the Union's blockading fleet.*

starve the Confederate armies and civil population into surrender.

During the Civil War and for the century which followed, many historians believed that the blockade of Southern ports was effective in crippling the Confederacy. "[W]ithout it," wrote James Russell Soley in 1887, "hostilities would have been protracted much longer, and would have been far more bitter and bloody than they were." Soley was a professor at the United States Naval Academy from 1871 to 1882, and served as assistant secretary of the United States Navy from 1890 to 1893. But modern historians disagree. Modern studies of the blockade suggest that the Union blockade did not strangle the South. Historians Robert Beringer, Herman Hattaway, Archer Jones, and William Still Jr., concluded in 1986 that "[T]here is much evidence that the blockade was not as critical to Confederate fortunes as many historians believe."

The first Lincoln blockade proclamation covered Southern ports from South Carolina, around Florida, and up to Texas. After Virginia and North Carolina left the Union, President Lincoln issued the second blockade proclamation on April 27, 1861, which extended the blockade to these states and up the Potomac River to Washington, D.C. Two Federal fleets were created for the Atlantic blockade, the North Atlantic Squadron and the South Atlantic Squadron. The Gulf of Mexico was also split between two Federal fleets.

It is interesting that throughout the Civil War, President Lincoln regarded the crisis as a rebellion. But by international law, his two blockade proclamations treated the Confederate States of America as a separate country at war with the United States. Foreign ships could not be turned back from entering Southern ports unless they were given official notice of the blockade. If foreign ships had no formal notice, they were allowed to continue into Confederate seaports. Likewise, foreign ships already in Southern harbors were given 15 days to leave.

Confederate and foreign ships tried to "run" the blockade during the four years of war. Generally, they were all very careful to follow international law: although the ships would try to run arms and ammunition into Rebel ports, they never used force against Union ships trying to stop them. Even when Federal warships fired at blockade-runners, the runners dared not fire back. Returning fire would have made them pirates under international law.

With its tiny navy of 1861, the Union committed itself to blockade 3,550 miles of Southern coastline and 189 Southern rivers from the Potomac River to the Rio Grande River in Texas. The job was almost impossible from the start. Just supporting four blockade squadrons was an enormous task: by the second year of the war, the steamships of the Union blockade were burning 3,000 tons of coal each week. The main Federal supply bases were at the seaports of Beaufort,

*The Confederate blockade-runner* Annie *tries to avoid capture near Wilmington, N.C.*

North Carolina; Port Royal, South Carolina; and Pensacola, Florida, and each of these ports had first to be captured from their Confederate defenders.

On both sides of the blockade, personal profit was a great inspiration. Under international law, Union navy sailors who captured merchant ships trying to run the blockade into Southern ports were entitled to share in the riches of every ship they captured. A captured blockade-runner was a "prize" under international law. Once a ship was captured, admiralty courts would set the value of that ship and its cargo bound for the Confederacy. The crew of the Union ship received one-half of that declared value to share among themselves. Any United States ship within eyeball range would also share in the prize money. Yankee crews shared the prize, and the runner's captured crew found themselves shipped north to prison at Fort Lafayette, New York.

Few blockade-runners sailed directly from Europe to Southern ports. Instead, they sailed to one of three islands off the Confederate coast. Other ships, usually small and fast, would run the blockade the rest of the way. The three main points between Europe and the Confederacy were Havana, Cuba; Nassau in the

*Sailors of the Union fleet chase a blockade-runner trying to sneak by in a storm.*

Bahama Islands; and Bermuda. From Cuba, the blockade-runners would head for Galveston, Texas; New Orleans; Mobile, Alabama; and St. Mark's, Florida. The Nassau ships would sail to Charleston, South Carolina; St. Augustine, Florida; Savannah, Georgia; or Wilmington, North Carolina. The Bermuda runners also sailed to the ports served by Nassau.

The largest and busiest blockade-runner port on the way to the South was Nassau. It was 500 miles from Savannah, 515 miles from Charleston, South Carolina, and 570 miles from Wilmington, North Carolina. Each trip could be made in three days by a fast steamer.

On December 5, 1861, the first blockade-runner leaving the Confederacy arrived at Nassau. The ship carried 144 bales of Southern cotton to be sold in England. With such cotton sales, the Confederacy hoped to purchase the weapons it needed to win independence. At Nassau in 1862, during the second year of the war, European factories were able to unload 200,000 weapons bound for the South. The South's greatest problem was not Yankee blockaders but available ships to run the blockade. There were only enough ships to transfer half of the weapons needed to the South in 1862. During the entire four-year war, the South only owned 11 blockade-runners. Hundreds of other ships had to be rented.

Blockade-running became a huge private business during the war. Ships registered in Europe and privately owned made the run across the Atlantic. Hundreds of British navy officers became captains of these ships. They had to use assumed names. Fortunes could be made. Sailors were paid up to $100 in gold per month plus a $50 bonus for each successful trip in or out of the South. Captains could make $5,000 gold every month. And if the cargo out of the South was cotton, the captain of the blockade-runner was allowed to keep five to ten bales for himself which he could sell in England.

As Stephen Wise of the University of South Carolina wrote, "Without profits, blockade running would not have existed." Profit was often based upon cotton. Blockade-runners could buy Confederate cotton for nine cents per bale and sell it in Nassau to English merchants for one dollar. The South also used cotton as collateral for European loans for buying arms and supplies. Loans were to be repaid in cotton at the rate of 12 cents per pound.

When foreign ships tried to run through the Union blockade, the runners usually carried private goods for sale in the South as well as war supplies for the Confederate government. Indeed, so much cargo space was used for private goods that the Confederate Congress in February 1864 passed a law forcing blockade-runners to use half their cargo space for war supplies. Before then, the blockade-runners usually used only one-third of their space for war materials. The rest would be civilian clothing and luxuries like perfume and candy.

Blockade-runners had to be fast and difficult to see if they hoped to outrun the Union blockade fleet waiting outside Southern harbors. The runners were painted light gray to be almost invisible on the ocean. To reduce their visible silhouettes, lifeboats were lowered near port and sail masts were cut in half. Even sailors wore white or gray clothing.

The first ship to run the Yankee blockade into the South was the *Bermuda*, a 211-foot-long steamer. She sailed from England on August 22, 1861, and reached Savannah, Georgia, on September 18. She carried 24,000 blankets for Confederate soldiers, at least 50,000 shoes, 22 cannons, 6,500 rifles, and 20,000 rifle cartridges. On October 29, she left Savannah to sail back to England with 2,000 bales of Confederate cotton. The *Bermuda* was finally captured by the blockade fleet near Nassau on April 27, 1862.

More than once, blockade-runners sailing to or from the South carried more than valuable cargo. They carried deadly disease. One blockade-runner left North Carolina for Nassau carrying both cotton and yellow fever. Between Wilmington and the island, 28 crewmen became sick and seven died. During the summer of 1864, a Nassau epidemic of yellow fever caused a 21-day quarantine of all ships docked there. The normal two-week round trip to Confederate ports then became two months, counting the quarantine delays.

Some blockade-runners made history. The runner *Banshee* was built in England specifically to run the Union blockade. She was 220 feet long, 20 feet wide, and was powered by sidewheels. She was the first all-steel ship to cross the Atlantic. Burning 30 tons of coal per day for her steam engines, she arrived at Nassau on April 20, 1863. From there, her captain, Jonathan

Steele, sailed to Wilmington, North Carolina, arriving on May 12 after a three-day voyage. The *Banshee* and Captain Steele became famous in the South when they made a run with an Arabian horse lashed to the main deck. The horse was a gift for President Jefferson Davis from Confederate business agents in Egypt. The *Banshee* made nine successful runs through the blockade before she was captured November 21, 1863.

Captain Louis M. Coxetter made 24 blockade runs from England to Nassau to Wilmington during 1862 and 1863. His ship the *Herald* was finally captured on December 20, 1863. Captain John Wilkinson commanded the steamer *Robert E. Lee* through the blockade 21 times before his ship was finally captured.

The South desperately needed European supplies and the Union blockade tried to stop them. Between April 1861 and July 1863, the South's few factories made 40,000 rifles, but the blockade-runners brought in another 200,000. In March through September of 1864, blockade-runners brought to the South 22,000 rifles, one million pounds of potassium nitrate (essential for making gunpowder), 300,000 pairs of shoes, and 275,000 blankets. During the second half of 1864, blockade-runners brought to just Charleston and Wilmington at least 500,000 pairs of shoes, 300,000 blankets, 3.5 million pounds of meat, 50,000 rifles, 43 cannons, and 2 million pounds of potassium nitrate.

Even though Union Admiral Farragut closed Mobile, Alabama, to blockade-runners in August 1864, 19 of 22 blockade-runners made it through the blockade before August. The Union blockade leaked everywhere. At the vital Confederate port city of Wilmington, North Carolina, there were 2,054 attempts to run the blockade. Of these, 1,735 made it. At the Confederate ports on the Gulf of Mexico, out of 2,960 attempts to run the blockade, 65 percent succeeded in 1862, 62 percent made it in 1863, 87 percent made it through in 1864, and in 1865, the war's last year, 94 percent of the blockade-runners got through.

By the end of the war, the South had managed to get 400,000 rifles through the blockade. The gray, sleek blockade-runners brought to the Confederacy 60 percent of the South's weapons, 33 percent of its lead for bullets, 75 percent of its ingredients for making gunpowder, and nearly all of the South's cloth and leather for its armies.

Even though 136 blockade-runners were captured and another 85 destroyed by the blockade squadrons, modern historians now believe that running the blockade was one campaign which the Confederacy won. However, things looked different to hungry, sick, and wounded Confederate soldiers and civilians when the Confederate States of America was under siege by land and by sea. The general success of the Rebel blockade-runners was a victory not seen by Private Carlton McCarthy in the Second Corps of Robert E. Lee's Army of Northern Virginia. As he remembered it: "The Confederate soldier fought a host of ills occasioned by the deprivation of chloroform and morphia which were excluded from the Confederacy by the blockade as contraband of war. The man who has submitted to amputation without chloroform or tossed on a couch of agony for a night and a day without sleep for want of a dose of morphia, may possibly be able to estimate the advantages which resulted from the possession by the federal surgeons of an unlimited supply of these."

In 1864, the coastlines of the South and the Mississippi River were not the only sites of naval conflicts of the Civil War. Rebels and Yankees would also do battle in the English Channel.

# V

# *War Across the Sea*

*A*lthough the *Monitor* and the *Virginia* (the *Merrimack*) are the two most famous ships of the Civil War, the second pair of most famous ships should be the USS *Kearsarge* and the CSS *Alabama*. They fought the most distant battle of the war—in the English Channel between France and England.

Confederate sea captain Raphael Semmes was born in Maryland and went to sea when he was 16. During the first two months of the Civil War, he went to sea in command of the Confederate steamer CSS *Sumter*. Semmes raided Yankee merchant ships and captured 18. Sailing to Europe, Semmes accepted his most famous command, the Rebel steamer CSS *Alabama*. Semmes spent two years intercepting Union merchant ships on the open ocean.

By June 1864, the *Alabama* and Captain Semmes had captured another 64 merchant ships flying the Union flag. Since the *Alabama* was a Confederate warship and not a blockade-runner, it carried cannons. It sank the Union warship USS *Hatteras* off Galveston, Texas, in January 1862. On June 11, 1864, the *Alabama*

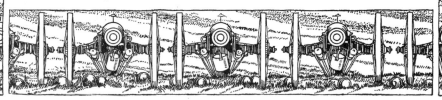

*The Civil War extended over the ocean when the CSS* Alabama *(above) fought the USS* Kearsage *in the waters off France.*

steamed into port at Cherbourg, France. Semmes had traveled 75,000 miles in 21 months.

Three days later, the United States warship USS *Kearsarge* anchored off Cherbourg harbor. Captain John A. Winslow stayed offshore to avoid violating international law by challenging the *Alabama* in waters belonging to France.

The *Kearsarge* and the *Alabama* were both steamships which used propellers. Both ships also carried masts and sails.

Confident that his wooden *Alabama* could sink the wooden *Kearsarge*, Captain Semmes decided to sail out and fight. On June 14, 1864, Semmes sent a formal letter to the Confederate business agent in Cherbourg for delivery to the United States consul to France, with instructions to relay the challenge to Captain Winslow: "I desire you to say to the U. S. Consul that my intention is to fight the *Kearsarge* as soon as I can make the necessary arrangements."

Captain Semmes did not know that the *Kearsarge* was almost an ironclad: Captain Winslow had covered the sides of the *Kearsarge* with 720 feet of 1.7-inch iron chains to block enemy cannonballs and shells. The chains were hidden behind 1-inch thick boards. Twenty-three years later, the executive officer on board the *Alabama* said of Captain Semmes's fight with the *Kearsarge*: "I will state that the battle would never have been fought had he known that the *Kearsarge* wore an armor of chain beneath her outer covering."

On Sunday morning, June 19, 1864, at 9:30, the *Alabama* steamed out of Cherbourg harbor to fight the *Kearsarge*. Behind the *Alabama* sailed the little steam yacht from England, the *Deerhound*. She flew the

*Captain John A. Winslow commanded the USS* Kearsage *in its fight with the CSS* Alabama.

*Captain Raphael Semmes jumped overboard with his crew as the CSS* Alabama *went to its watery grave.*

ensign of the Royal Mersey Yacht Club.

On shore, at least 15,000 spectators watched the *Alabama* sail seven miles out to sea where the *Kearsarge* waited. The Frenchmen could see which ship was which by its smoke: the *Alabama*'s boilers burned coal from Wales and the *Kearsarge* burned coal from England. Their smoke looked different.

By 11:10, the ships were seven miles out. The *Alabama* fired her cannons from 1,200 yards away and closed to within 900 yards of the *Kearsarge*. Both ships began sailing along the same circular path, half a mile apart. They circled to their right (starboard), each ship firing her starboard-side cannons at the other. On sailing ships of the day, steam and sail, turning the ship's steering wheel to *port* (left) turned the ship to the opposite side—*starboard* or right. Since both the *Kearsarge* and the *Alabama* steered to starboard, their steering wheels were thrown to port. For this reason, some historians make the mistake of stating that their common circle was sailed to port, leftward, when only the steering wheels were swung left to make the ships turn right.

The *Alabama*'s shot and shell bounced off the *Kearsarge*'s chain armor. Each ship fired furiously, the *Alabama* firing her seven starboard cannons and the *Kearsarge*'s five starboard guns answering. Continuing on their circular path, they made seven slow circles.

By noon, the *Kearsarge* had fired 173 rounds and the *Alabama* had answered with more than 300. But it was the CSS *Alabama* that was sinking.

At 12:15 at the beginning of their eighth circle, the *Alabama* lowered her flag, the international symbol of surrender at sea. Brave sailors on the *Alabama* who refused to surrender fired one more cannon and the *Kearsarge* had to answer by firing a round at the sinking ship. The cannons did not fire again. The *Alabama* was sinking fast, stern first. As the crew jumped into the sea, Captain Semmes threw his sword into the

Harper's Weekly's *depiction of the sinking of the CSS* Alabama *and the rescue of its crew.*

water and then jumped with his crew. The *Alabama* sank in 20 minutes.

The little steam yacht *Deerhound* sailed near the *Kearsarge*. Her captain remembered hearing Captain Winslow shout, "For God's sake, do what you can to save them."

The *Deerhound* and lifeboats from the *Kearsarge* picked up the *Alabama*'s survivors. The *Deerhound* picked up Captain Semmes and escaped with him to England so the Confederate captain would not be captured with his crew.

The *Kearsarge* picked up six officers and 64 sailors from the water. Twenty of them were wounded and three would die. Of the *Alabama*'s crew, nine men died, another 10 drowned when they abandoned ship, and 21 were wounded.

Three men were wounded on the *Kearsarge*. Gunner John W. Dempsey lost his arm. Seaman William Gowin from Michigan had his leg shattered when a cannon shell blew through the armor chains. He refused to allow his fellow sailors to leave their hot cannons to help him. Gowin died of his wounds in a French hospital. Captain Winslow called the dead seaman "a brave and gallant sailor."

The *Alabama*'s 300 cannon rounds struck the *Kearsarge* 28 times during the 65-minute battle. One 100-pound shell failed to explode when it slammed into the stern of the *Kearsarge*. When Abraham Lincoln heard of the victory in the English Channel and of the unexploded shell stuck in the stern post of the *Kearsarge*, the president wanted the shell as a trophy. On January 28, 1865, the commandant of the Boston Navy Yard dug the dud shell out of the *Kearsarge* and sent the shell to Navy Secretary Gideon Welles for President Lincoln.

From April 1861 to April 1865, the seafaring nations of the world closely watched the American Civil War. They studied the war's advances in military science and technology. Of all the Civil War lessons which nations took with them into the 20th century, none were more important than the development of fast merchant ships and armored warships.

Pook's turtles on the Mississippi River would become the massive dreadnaughts of the First World War and the huge Missouri-class battlewagons of the Second World War. But they all began in 1861 with John Ericsson's little wooden model of an unseaworthy cheese box on a raft, which he had named the *Monitor*.

# Glossary

| | |
|---|---|
| *blockade* | A military maneuver in which supply and information sources are cut off to a city or harbor. |
| *blockade-runners* | Ships used to race through the enemy line of blockading ships in harbors or on rivers. |
| *bluecoats* | Term used for soldiers in the Northern Union army during the Civil War because of the color of their uniforms. |
| *Confederacy* | The Confederate States of America; the South. |
| *Confederate* | Citizen of the Confederate States of America; a Southerner during the Civil War. |
| *draft* | Pertaining to a ship, how deep in the water a ship floats. |
| *Federals* | A name used for members of the Union. |
| *graycoats* | Term used for soldiers in the Southern Confederate army during the Civil War because of the color of their uniforms. |
| *ironclad* | A wooden ship covered in iron armor. |
| *paddle wheel* | A large wheel attached to the sides or back of a ship that has paddles all around it to help propel the ship. |
| *Rebels* | Term used for Southerners in the Civil War. |
| *secessionist* | Southerners who voted to secede from the Union and form their own republic. |
| *tinclad* | Smaller riverboat covered with a thinner plate of iron than an ironclad. |
| *Union* | The United States of America; the North. |
| *Yankees* | Term used for Northerners during the Civil War. |

# Further Reading

Ammen, Daniel. *The Atlantic Coast*. Charles Scribner's Sons, NY, 1883.

Carse, Robert. *Blockade: The Civil War at Sea*. Rinehart and Company, NY, 1958.

Cushing, William B. "The Destruction of the *Albemarle*," *Battles and Leaders*, IV. The Century, NY, 1889.

Ericsson, John, "The Building of the *Monitor*," *Battles and Leaders*, I. The Century, NY, 1887.

Greene, Jack, and Alessandro Massignani. *Ironclads at War: The Origin and Development of the Armored Warship*, 1854-1891. Combined Publishing, Conshohocken, PA, 1998.

Greene, S. Dana. "In the *Monitor's* Turret," *Battles and Leaders*, I. The Century, NY, 1887.

Kell, John M. "Cruise and Combats of the *Alabama*," *Battles and Leaders*, IV. The Century, NY, 1889.

Kinney, John C. "Farragut at Mobile Bay," *Battles and Leaders*, IV. The Century, NY, 1889.

Rogers, C. R. P. "DuPont's Attack at Charleston," *Battles and Leaders*, IV. The Century, NY, 1889.

Soley, James Russell. *The Blockade and the Cruisers*. Charles Scribner's Sons, NY, 1887.

_____. "The Union and Confederate Navies," *Battles and Leaders*, I. The Century, NY, 1887.

West, Richard S., Jr. *Mr. Lincoln's Navy*. Longmans, Green and Company, NY, 1957.

Wise, Stephen R. *Lifeline of the Confederacy: Blockade Running During the Civil War*. University of South Carolina Press, Columbia, SC, 1988.

Wood, John Taylor. "The First Fight of Ironclads," *Battles and Leaders*, I. The Century, NY, 1887.

# Websites About Ironclads and Blockades in the Civil War

Civil War Era Gunboats and Monitors:
   http://www.uss-salem.org/features/nara/gun-mon.htm
Civil War Navies:
   http://www.wtj.com/archives/acwnavies/
Confederate States Navy; Museum, Library and Research Institute:
   http://www.csnavy.org/
Department of the Navy, Naval Historical Center:
   http://www.history.navy.mil/index.html
Ironclads and Blockade-Runners of the American Civil War:
   http://www.ameritech.net/users/maxdemon/
   ironclads.htm

# Index

# INDEX

## PHOTO CREDITS

*Harper's Weekly*: pp. 12, 18, 24, 29, 34, 36, 40, 41, 45, 47, 48, 54, 55, 56, 57; Library of Congress: pp. 20, 26, 32; National Archives: pp. 13, 15, 17, 39; United States Army Military History Institute: p. 10